Original title:
Ode to the Peace Lily

Copyright © 2025 Creative Arts Management OÜ
All rights reserved.

Author: Mariana Leclair
ISBN HARDBACK: 978-1-80581-740-6
ISBN PAPERBACK: 978-1-80581-267-8
ISBN EBOOK: 978-1-80581-740-6

The Quiet Heart of Indoor Gardens

In the corner, she's a sight,
Greenest queen, a pure delight.
With petals soft, she holds her ground,
In silence, laughter can be found.

Dusty leaves, a timid face,
Whispers secrets in her space.
She nods when I spill my tea,
Always judging, never free.

Mysteries in the Verdant Silence

What does she know, that leafy sage?
In her world, I'm just a page.
Plants don't gossip, or do they lie?
Peeking at me with a knowing eye.

Grow your roots and make a stand,
But never lend a helping hand.
In her green, the truth ignites,
She's the queen of indoor fights!

A Floral Whisper to the World

Hey there, lily, don't you frown,
Your blooms will never let you drown.
With every leaf, you crack a grin,
Just waiting for my next chagrin.

You catch my woes, a silent friend,
Yet still you mock; oh, it won't end.
In fairy tales, you'd steal the show,
But in this house? You steal the glow!

Soft Glow of Presence

In the corner, a plant does sit,
With leaves like fans, it's a real hit.
Water it softly, not too much please,
Or it'll throw a fit and sneeze like the breeze.

Its blooms are white, a pure little sight,
It knows how to shine, but not too bright.
With a wink of green, it sometimes sways,
In the corner of rooms, it frolics all day.

A Tranquil Soul's Farewell.

Oh, gentle leaf of calming hue,
You bring peace where chaos grew.
Even in storms, you stand so tall,
A warrior of calm against the brawl.

With each droop, you tell a tale,
Of watered hopes that seem to fail.
But with sunlight, you're up again,
Laughing at the world, in your leafy den.

Whispers of the Serene Blossom

In the quiet dusk, it starts to show,
A dance of leaves, like soft marshmallow.
Whispers of green, oh what a sight,
Poking fun at my unkempt fright!

Its flowers nod, a sweet delight,
At my messy desk, they take a flight.
They laugh at papers scattered wide,
While I just sigh and try to hide.

Guardian of Tranquil Spaces

With the grace of a ninja, it stands so bold,
In the corner of rooms, it's a sight to behold.
It guards my thoughts and my caffeinated cup,
While I glance at Facebook, oh here we go up!

Should I forget to water, it silently pouts,
Though a little droop gets my focus about.
With a spritz and a smile, we're pals once more,
Oh, guardian green, who could want more?

In the Arms of Nature

In the corner of the room, it sways,
A leafy dancer in a light, warm haze.
It shimmies with grace, what a sight to see,
Catching dust bunnies like it's on a spree.

Seems to know the secrets of chill and grace,
Whispering calm like it owns this place.
While I trip over shoes, it just rolls its eyes,
Telling me, 'Breathe deep,' as it reaches for the skies.

Echoes of Peace Abloom

A peace lily laughing, oh, what a tease,
Bobbing its head like it's missed the breeze.
'Why so serious?' it seems to exclaim,
As I juggle my worries, a comical game.

With blooms so white, it brings me delight,
While it silently plots to keep me upright.
It sips on my coffee, or maybe my fears,
A soft-spoken sage who dispels all my tears.

The Soul's Gentle Companion

In my chaotic world, you stand so serene,
With leaves like green umbrellas, you're my little queen.
You throw shade like a boss, while I stress and fret,
But then, you just droop, and I feel the regret.

As I talk to you daily, like you understand,
You nod with your leaves like a gentle hand.
While I worry about life, you simply bloom,
A partner in chaos, dispelling the gloom.

Fragrance of Calmness

Whiff of calm in the air like a sweet perfume,
In your leafy embrace, I forget all the doom.
You seem to giggle when I spill my tea,
Saying, 'Don't fret, my friend, just let it be!'

In laughter and light, we share our space,
You brighten my mornings, keeping up the pace.
If only I could grow roots to your peace,
But for now, I'll just dance, and let joy increase.

Beneath the Shadow of Grace

In corners dim, where you reside,
With petals bright, you take great pride.
You wave your leaves, a gentle tease,
Whispering secrets of the breeze.

Oh, comical bloom, your moves so sly,
Staying still, yet reaching high.
You act all shy, but we all know,
You're the star of the show, taking a bow.

Your pot is home, a cozy space,
Yet somehow, you flaunt with grace.
With every sip, you show your thirst,
And in your presence, I might burst!

So here's a toast, my leafy friend,
To your antics that never end.
Beneath your shade, I find my muse,
Let's dance, dear plant, or just refuse!

Keeper of Quiet Spaces

In the stillness, you stand tall,
A leafy guardian, over all.
You guard my thoughts with leafy flair,
While I pretend, you're just a chair.

Your serene vibe, it makes me think,
Of all the times I spilled my drink.
You don't complain; you just absorb,
I've lost the count of my clumsy chore.

You watch me fret, and roll my eyes,
As cats parade with stealthy sighs.
Yet, you just beam with peaceful glee,
Like you're the queen, and I, the bee.

So in this space, let laughter ring,
With your quiet charm, a soothing thing.
Though I may trip and stub my toe,
With you around, good vibes just flow!

A Dance of Pure Simplicity

Oh, the elegance in your stance,
You don't need a flashy dance.
With a little twist and a calm sigh,
You sway like you're in a lullaby.

In my kitchen, you reign supreme,
Mocking the chaos, living the dream.
You laugh while I make a big mess,
But you don't care; you're just impressed.

You bow your head in the afternoon sun,
While I juggle tasks, trying to run.
Yet there you are, with timeless ease,
You take your time, as if to tease.

So here's to simplicity, pure and bright,
In your presence, all feels right.
I tip my hat to your green parade,
Father Time's jealous; you've got it made!

Surrender to the Silent Bloom

With petals white, you stand so still,
In the chaos of life, you're quite the thrill.
You watch my coffee spill and stain,
And laugh at my struggles, all in vain.

In your calm arms, I find reprieve,
While every ounce of sense I weave.
You listen well, with no advice,
Just nurture in silence, a gentle spice.

You sway with grace when the winds blow,
While I trip on toys, spilling woe.
Yet, in your bloom, there's silent cheer,
You nod and smile; it's all too clear.

So here's to you, my quiet muse,
With every glance, you never lose.
I'll surrender to your silent glow,
Dancing on floors I dare not show!

The Whispering Sanctuary

In corners where you linger,
A secret joke you keep.
Your leaves do dance like ballerinas,
In silence, they do leap.

Your pot's a cozy cradle,
For thoughts to twist and twirl.
I swear I heard you chuckle,
As I tripped on a curl.

Beneath the sun you sparkle,
A diva in the light.
Did you just wink at Fido?
Oh, what a sight, what a sight!

In our little kingdom,
You rule with leafy grace.
I'll bow to your green wisdom,
In this whimsical space.

Nature's Solace in Bloom

With petals pure and glowing,
You mock my daily grind.
Your serene little strut,
Leaves my worries behind.

I dub you Queen of Quiet,
Yet you spill such pure glee.
Did you just roll your eyes?
You must be teasing me!

A household rebel, you bloom,
With grace and cheeky flair.
Is that a smirk I'm seeing?
Oh, do you really care?

From morning's light to starlit night,
You bask in aura bright.
A jester dressed in green,
Oh, what a funny sight!

Luminous Presence of Stillness

In the stillness of your presence,
You steal the show, oh dear!
Your calm's a gentle whisper,
With a grin that brings good cheer.

Oh, how you sway so gently,
As if to say, 'Let's play!'
Your heart is pure tranquility,
Yet mischief's on display.

With every bloom you flaunt,
You sprinkle joy around.
I think you're up to something,
My peaceful little mound.

When life gets loud and rambunctious,
You stand there, oh so cool.
A giggling green magician,
In this chaotic pool!

Unfurling the Essence of Peace

As you unfurl your blossoms,
A comical surprise!
Like a magician's handkerchief,
Appearing before my eyes.

You sit upon the table,
With regal poise and flair.
I swear you wink at neighbors,
As if they're unaware.

Your leaves are playful whispers,
Sharing secrets, oh so sly.
Do you think you're smarter?
You're the queen; I'm the pie!

In this dance of daily bliss,
You hold the laughter tight.
With humor in your petals,
You brighten up the night!

The Quiet Guardian of My Space

In the corner, a lily stands tall,
Whispers secrets, won't share them all.
Dust floats by, she gives me a glare,
Such a diva, with roots and flair.

Hiding from sunshine, she pleads for peace,
While I water, her demands increase.
A little too quiet, with her leafy grin,
Keep your gossip, I'm here to win!

Still Waters and Peaceful Flowers

In my room, she plays the judge,
With soft green leaves, she won't budge.
Loves her quiet, don't touch the pot,
She'll thrive even if I forget the spot!

With each glance, she nods and beams,
Sipping sunshine with great memes.
Her idea of fun is a dust-free shelf,
I chuckle; peace, but at what cost to myself?

Dance of the Leafy Sentinels

Oh, the leafy dance in the glowing light,
The lily sways, oh what a sight!
She'll judge my taste in plant décor,
But her elegance leaves me wanting more.

With every breeze, she nearly prances,
As if in tune, with all her chances.
Yet when I water, she rolls her eyes,
"Could you be gentler?" Oh, the sighs!

The Graceful Euphony of Verdant Life

Her leaves make music when shaken light,
Funny rhythms, they dance with delight.
"Less drama, more water!" I hear her plea,
As if she's conducting a green symphony!

She's the queen of calm in my clumsy space,
Rolling her eyes while I trip and race.
With chlorophyll charm, she steals the show,
Who knew peace could have such a glow?

Flora's Serenade Under Soft Skies

In a pot of laughter, she grows so bright,
Waving leaves like fans, what a silly sight.
Neighbors wonder if she throws a party,
With greenery dressed up, oh so hearty!

A dance on the windowsill, she sways with glee,
Beguiled by the light, who could disagree?
When the cat strolls by, she gives a wink,
While giving all of us time to think.

With petals a'flutter, she starts to hum,
Imitating the rhythm of a distant drum.
She giggles with sunlight that peeks through the pane,
Wishing for rain, oh, what a refrain!

Mirthful whispers float through this sweet space,
Our leafy friend's chuckles leave quite the trace.
So let's raise a glass to her cheerful charms,
This flora, so playful, with soothing arms.

The Sanctuary of Calm Blooms

In the corner of the room, she sits with flair,
An amusing little blossom, beyond compare.
She throws her leaves like confetti, it seems,
Welcoming you home from your daytime dreams.

Each stem is a giggle, each leaf is a grin,
Her whispers of joy always pull you in.
With friends of her kind, she throws a show,
A comedy of colors, what a lovely glow!

When the wind gently blows, she starts a dance,
Spinning round and round, what a silly prance.
All tomatoes envy her joyous scene,
In this sanctuary, she reigns like a queen.

Laughter is shared in this botanical space,
With petals and smiles, we all find our place.
She guards the room with a funny little pout,
In the kingdom of blooms, there's nothing to doubt!

Solace Beneath the Leaf

Beneath her leafy roof, we gather 'round,
Where crickets and laughter can always be found.
With a wink and a nod, she brightens the gloom,
Wearing a crown made of petals in bloom.

She listens intently as the jokes unfold,
Turning silence to warmth like a story told.
When the dog prances in, she rolls her gaze,
A sly little smirk in her leafy ways.

Sunshine spills in, making shadows play,
Her presence a joy that brightens the day.
It's a comedy club with chlorophyll flair,
Beneath her green watch, we shed every care.

So here's to the peace under leaves soft and wide,
Her humor and grace, our fondest guide.
In this leafy abode, we're ever a team,
A sanctuary of laughter, a botanical dream!

Silent Harmony in Nature's Realm

In a world of banter, she stands so still,
Cracking the sylvan silence with a cheerful thrill.
Her whispers collide with the buzzing delight,
Every bloom a soft joke, every color a light.

With a touch of mischief, she sprinkles her cheer,
In the laughter of petals, she draws us near.
When raindrops fall, she gives a chuckle or two,
Embracing the soggy, she knows what to do.

Underneath her broad leaves, secrets abide,
Nature's own jester, with her arms open wide.
While squirrels scuttle, she gives a soft wave,
Cleaning up the mess, she's our little brave.

So lift up your spirits, let joy take its flight,
In this gallery of peace, everything feels right.
With flora's own quirk, we smile and we dream,
Together with her laughter, nothing's as it seems!

A Hymn for Indoor Gardens

In the corner, a plant does sway,
A leafy friend who just loves to play.
Whispers of green in a sunny spot,
Growing so tall, but it's still a tot.

Jokes with the dust bunnies, having a blast,
A quiet party, and it's not too fast.
Leaves doing the tango, pots full of cheer,
Mellow vibes only, no room for fear.

Water it once, and its love will bloom,
Give it some sunlight, watch it consume.
No need for a gardener, just some good wit,
This leafy delight is a real hit!

So here's to the plants in our cozy rooms,
Bringing us joy as they dance and loom.
A funny little friend, so no need to fuss,
In this indoor garden, it's just us.

The Serenade of the Pure Bloom

Swaying to music from the fridge's hum,
A pure white bloom that makes my heart thrum.
It doesn't judge, just wants a friend,
With gentle vibes, on it I depend.

Sunshine's its partner, water's its dance,
In the living room, it takes a chance.
Sipping on light, with such great finesse,
No drama here, just a peaceful mess.

Bet it can talk, if only it could,
Sharing the secrets of the house it would.
A giggling flower, with petals so bright,
Making my mornings feel just right!

So, here's to the quiet, bold little sprout,
In a world of chaos, it's what life's about.
A silly serenade, just follow the tune,
In the heart of the home, it's the best cartoon.

Peace's Gentle Emissary

In the corner stands a peace-keeper,
With green as tranquil as a well-loved sleeper.
A gentle whisper, a calming sight,
Letting out giggles in the soft moonlight.

Not one to fret about dirt or grime,
Just happily growing, every single time.
Leaves like umbrellas, sheltering all,
A friend for the tropics, in a cozy hall.

Every glance sends a smile your way,
A tiny comedian, here to stay.
With sprigs of joy and a wink of green,
The calmest jester you've ever seen.

So, let's raise a toast to this quirky sage,
Bringing warm laughter at every stage.
With a nod and a grin, it nods back too,
A peace-loving pal, just for you.

The Calming Artistry of Leaves

In a pot of dreams, where laughter ignites,
A dance of the leaves under soft, golden lights.
Spreading good vibes with a twirl and a smile,
Exuding a calm that's just so worthwhile.

No need for a stage, it's a star all alone,
With every new leaf, it claims its throne.
Whispers of green that play hide and seek,
Decorating the home, there's no need to speak.

Promising peace with each gentle sway,
It's like having fun, in its leafy ballet.
Cracking jokes with the breeze every night,
A calming artistry, taking flight.

So when you feel stressed in your daily race,
Look over to this friend, it's full of grace.
A leaf-laden buddy, bringing delight,
With laughter and joy, it's pure, not a fright.

Petals of Calm in a Chaotic World

In a room with shoes and socks,
A peace lily stands, counting rocks.
Lost among laundry's wild spree,
It whispers, "Hey, just be with me."

While chaos reigns like a circus clown,
This plant won't let you wear a frown.
With petals soft, it's quite the tease,
"I'll cheer you up! Just breathe with ease."

In the mess of life, it plays its part,
With silent wisdom, a calming art.
It sways gently in the breeze,
Saying, "Dance now, life's a tease!"

So here's to you, dear leafy friend,
You've got a charm that won't soon end.
Through tangled cords and cluttered sights,
Your quirky grace brings endless flights.

The Guardian of the Indoor Breeze

In the corner stands a leafy knight,
Guarding breezes with all its might.
While dust bunnies plot, oh what a fright,
It laughs, pollinating the light!

A sentinel of calm, a spectral sprite,
Battling chaos with sheer delight.
"Why so serious?" it seems to say,
"Let's chillax, relax, it's a flower play!"

With a wink, it sways in its pot,
Counting the smiles, it's quite a lot.
"For every sigh, I'll give you cheer,
Just breathe it in, my flower dear!"

Oh noble plant, you wear no crown,
Yet rule the air when troubles drown.
With gentle grace, you spread the tease,
As the world jitters, you bring the ease.

Nurtured by the Light

A peace lily basking in the glow,
With sunlight's kiss, it's quite the show.
"Another plant? Oh, what a fright!
But look at me, I'm pure delight!"

With sassy leaves, it strikes a pose,
"Do I need water? Who knows, who knows!"
A splash here and there, just a quick fling,
"Life's too short for the dull and bland spring!"

It leans toward the window, seeking that sun,
"Just a few rays, and I'll have my fun!"
With every beam, a playful dance,
Inviting all for a glance, a chance.

So here's to you, my green delight,
Nurtured well, you shine so bright.
In quirky spills of potting dirt,
You giggle soft in your leafy skirt.

In the Shade of Gentle Leaves

In the shade where laughter hides,
A peace lily giggles, it never hides.
"Beneath my leaves, come take a seat,
I promise you, life's a silly beat!"

Every petal a secret, softly spun,
"It's picnic time, we'll have some fun!"
A tea party with dust and little bugs,
It smiles widely, passing out hugs.

With roots strong, it knows the game,
Making the mundane, never the same.
"Let's share stories of shoes and socks,
In this crazy world, I'll be your fox!"

So lean on me, my leafy friend,
With gentle shade right up to the end.
In this bizarre dance of plant and host,
You're the one I cherish most.

A Canvas of Tranquility

In a pot with roots like spaghetti,
A lily stands, calm and steady.
It whispers truths, but I'm not sure,
If peace arrived or just a blur.

With leaves that dance like they are tipsy,
It sways around, acting quite frisky.
I swear it winked with its glossy sheen,
And asked me if I've ever seen.

The Gentle Wave of Nature's Touch

A leaf so wide, it could be a sail,
A tiny boat on a breeze's trail.
In the wind, it swishes and glides,
Waving at neighbors, never hides.

It pulls off cool like a classy star,
While my houseplants just blend and spar.
Sometimes I think it's plotting and scheming,
Conspiring against my peaceful dreaming.

A Tribute to Pure Serenity

Oh, tranquil friend in sunny spots,
You rally joy, though life's big knots.
I chat with you while sipping tea,
You nod along unconditionally.

I thought I saw you blush today,
With that cute little leaf display.
Could it be you enjoy my chatter?
Or just pretend, as if it's all a matter?

Gift of the Peaceful Blossom

In your white gown, you're all dressed up,
Like a fancy guest in a teacup.
You radiate smiles, not a bit shy,
Cracking jokes, or is that just my eye?

You truce with dust and pair with grime,
Throwing sass without a single rhyme.
A blossom with attitude, oh-so-brave,
In your presence, boredom just won't save.

The Allure of Stillness

In corners it quietly sits,
A leaf so smooth, free of bits.
With elegance, it takes the stage,
It's the star on Nature's page.

People walk by and say, 'Wow!'
"Where's your party? Show us how!"
But peace just smiles, and stays so cool,
Teaching us to chill, like a fool.

With waters sipped in tranquil grace,
A soft reminder, it's not a race.
In its presence, I just can't frown,
It's like wearing a calm, leafy crown.

So here's to the plant that plays it low,
While others jump, and others glow.
Let's bow to its tranquil scene,
The most serene, leafy green machine!

The Breeze's Quiet Dance

Whispers glide on gentle air,
As leaves sway without a care.
A twist, a turn, a playful sweep,
In this dance, the world feels deep.

The breeze comes by for a little chat,
"Don't you worry, where's your hat?"
The lily nods, with no alarm,
"Just let me be, I'll bring the calm."

In soft pirouettes, it spins around,
A plant so chill, it's unbound.
With petals white, it shows no haste,
While I'm just here, with cookies placed.

"Shall we groove?" the breeze inquires,
"I think I'll just sit and retire."
And so the lily lounges proud,
While nature hums an airy crowd.

Nature's Ambassadors of Calm

Oh little lily, a chill diplomat,
With a vibe so cool, it makes me chat.
"Is life a rush?" I curiously ask,
"Not today, dear friend, that's not my task."

It waves its leaves, like a gentle hand,
"Just breathe it in, let life be grand."
While I dodge chaos, it winks with glee,
"I'm here for laughs, come sip some tea!"

Pictures of zen, they take their place,
Helping us all to slow the pace.
A meeting of minds in the still of night,
"Let's write this song—melody bright!"

So here's to the peace, so graceful and shy,
With every glance, it catches the eye.
In laughter, it grows, so timeless and neat,
A plant that dances, now isn't that sweet?

The Dance of Tenderness

Have you seen the leaves bounce and sway?
As if they're saying, "Come out and play!"
With a tip-toe and twirl, they leap in the light,
Now isn't that quite a charming sight?

Laughter surrounds in a leafy embrace,
It's like this plant understands our pace.
With every breath, it molds the air,
"Chillax, my friend, there's nothing rare!"

The petals chuckle, a soft little tease,
"Why rush when you can sway with ease?"
So I join in, with a silly little prance,
Paying homage in this fun, leafy dance.

Harmony flows, as giggles resound,
In a world where calmness oft can't be found.
So here's to the tenderness, soft as a sigh,
Let's dance in stillness, you and I!

Petals of Persuasion

In the corner she stands, dressed in white,
A leafy diva, a thrilling sight.
Whispers to me, 'Water me right!'
I chuckle and nod, she's my leafy knight.

With elegance poised, she sways with flair,
Mocking my plants that just don't care.
They wilt and droop, full of despair,
While she struts around, full of fresh air.

Her petals say, 'I'm not just for show,'
But can't help but laugh as I watch her glow.
She rolls her eyes at the cactus row,
Saying, 'Bloom with charm, let your colors flow!'

So here's to the lady, the peace lily queen,
With a joke in her leaves, she's forever green.
In this botanic soap opera scene,
She's the star who makes my home serene.

A Ritual of Renewal

Every Monday, a tiny parade,
With my peace lily, we've got it made.
She gives a nod, encourages the trade,
I bring her water, and together we invade.

The dust bunnies fear her clean, bright leaf,
They tremble in corners, filled with grief.
Every spurt of growth is beyond belief,
As I dance around, sharing joy, not a thief.

'Let's freshen up!' I shout with cheer,
She's sprouting new leaves, it's that time of year.
With each little sprout, I toast with a beer,
To the lily of peace—let's spread good cheer!

Together we laugh, a quirky duo,
My plant's my buddy; that's how we grow.
In this weekly ritual, we both know,
With a dash of green, life's a fun show!

Embracing the Quietude

In a room so still, she sways on her stalk,
A drama queen in whispers, doesn't talk.
Her leafy gestures leave me in shock,
As I sip my tea and ponder a rock.

"Are you done growing?" I tease with a grin,
She winks with a leaf that's saved up within.
In peaceful silence, she pulls me in,
To embrace the calm where the giggles begin.

Her wisdom—just breathe, let the chaos flee,
Staring at me, oh such tranquility!
Yet I can't help but wonder, goodie,
Is she plotting with my cat, just wait and see?

In her quietude, a laugh's dormant seed,
I'm sure she's raucous, just waiting to lead.
With every day's pause, I find she's agreed,
To plant joy in corners, that's her hidden creed.

The Soul of the Room

In a crowded space, she steals the scene,
A diva of foliage, crisp and clean.
Other plants sigh with a hint of green,
While she beams bright, like a laughing machine.

"Move over, sunshine!" she seems to tease,
With a shimmer of peace, she plays with ease.
Making my heart dance, like gentle breeze,
In her company, I'm never to freeze.

The dust clouds gather, but she doesn't fret,
With a wink of her leaf, she's not done yet.
To be the soul of the room is her bet,
So I pour her drink—she's a queen, I'll fret!

When guests arrive, they're drawn to her grace,
"Oh, what a plant!" they admire her face.
I just smile, knowing she's won her place,
In the tale of my home, a warm, snug embrace.

Heirloom of Harmony

In the corner it sits, a plant of such grace,
Its leaves wave hello, a green, leafy face.
It silently judges my watering skills,
With a smirk, it waits for its cup to fill.

When sunlight dances, it leans with delight,
A diva in green, showing off its bright.
Yet when I forget, oh what a scene,
Droopy and sad, like a drama queen.

With each gentle breeze, it answers my calls,
In a house full of chaos, it never falls.
Loyal and charming, my plant friend so dear,
With blooms like a carpet, no need for a sphere.

So here's to the lily, that grows with such cheer,
In the garden of laughter, it's the top tier.
In this heirloom of harmony, it plays its part,
A soft little jester, a green work of art.

Serene Whispers of Green

In the kitchen it lurks, a peace-loving sage,
Whispering secrets, it's quite the backstage.
With every new shoot, it giggles and croons,
Saying, "Water me well, and we'll dance to the tunes!"

Rooted in silence, it enjoys all the jest,
A plant with no worries, it smiles at the rest.
While I fret and I fumble, trying to thrive,
It just rolls its leaves, feeling quite alive.

It absorbs all my woes like a sponge with a grin,
Commiserating softly, sharing my din.
With blossoms like pillows, so fluffy and light,
They tickle my troubles, a comical sight.

Each time I water, I'm met with a tease,
Grinning, it sways in the freshest breeze.
In my home of a thousand, it's the queen who's seen,
In these serene whispers, it reigns evergreen.

Cradle of Stillness

In the nook of the room, it cradles my dreams,
With a tranquil demeanor, it's bursting at seams.
While I rush and I tumble through life's crazy maze,
It just stands there calmly, in its leafy phase.

Sometimes I catch it, mid-plant meditation,
While I stress and I stew, it's in sweet relaxation.
As I scurry about, bringing chaos and fun,
It smiles in stillness, the zen master won.

With petals like whispers and leaves soft as pie,
It knows all my secrets, oh my! Oh my!
In the cradle of stillness, it guides on my way,
A plant of pure patience, come laugh with me, stay.

So I tip my hat to this funny green friend,
Who shows me the art of a serene blend.
In a world that's too noisy, it quietly sings,
In this wild plant circus, it's the star with the bling.

In the Heart of a Modern Sanctuary

In the heart of my home, it plants its sweet roots,
A guardian of calm, in all the high-tech hoots.
While gadgets do beep and the screens glow so bright,
It keeps me grounded, in soft, gentle light.

With leaves that are glossy, like nature's finest art,
It mocks all my selfies, oh, it knows its part.
Each click of my camera is met with a glance,
"Take me from this scene; I'd rather have plants dance!"

When I ponder my future, it nods in agreement,
Unlike other devices, it's not on a screen yet.
All my worries dissolve in its peaceful embrace,
With humor and charm, it lightens the space.

So here's to my lily, my silent delight,
A partner in laughter, both day and at night.
In the heart of this sanctuary, both bright and alive,
With roots of compassion, it helps me thrive.

Sanctuary in Green

In a pot that's full of cheer,
A plant with leaves so grand and clear,
It waves its arms, a leafy cheerleader,
Saying, "Dust me off, you lazy feeder!"

With roots as strong as a crafty thief,
Stealing water, spreading leaf,
While I'm here, sipping tea with glee,
This plant makes growing seem so easy!

It whispers truth in the light of day,
"I'm low maintenance!" it seems to say,
While I drown in care, with each mist spray,
It stands there, swaying, in its own ballet!

Oh green delight, a silent friend,
In your stillness, I find the blend,
Of laughter wrapped in every leaf,
You're the peace I seek, my comic relief!

Serenity's Emissary

With petals white as winter's light,
It fails to judge my morning fright,
As I stumble through the sleepy scene,
This plant just beams, a bright machine!

Its only task is to absorb,
The sunshine, like a peaceful lord,
While I trip over shoes, oh dear,
It stands so still, with no fear near!

"Let's dance!" it whispers in the breeze,
While I negotiate my daily sneeze,
A healthy laugh is what I need,
Hey plant, let's partner in this deed!

So here's to you, my leafy mate,
You thrive despite my careless fate,
In your serene and funny way,
You transform my chaos into play!

The Flower of Quiet Resilience

In corners where the light is shy,
A warrior rests, beneath the sky,
It guards my peace with potted might,
While I freak out over laundry fight!

Though I might burn the toast each morn,
This plant stays cool, without a scorn,
It shrugs off drama, wearing leaf,
While I wear worry like a motif!

"Take a chill, my friend," it sighs,
"I'm here to help you face your fries,"
While I'm cooking chaos in the lane,
It's sipping sun, enjoying the gain!

Oh flower of calm, you clever sage,
With every day, you write a page,
In stories of laughter, you play your role,
A silent hero for my tired soul!

Caress of the Moonlit Petal

When the moon dips low, I see you glow,
In the night's embrace, your leaves just flow,
"Don't worry," they wink, "we're cool and fine,
As long as you offer us some sunshine!"

With your white blooms, a playful jest,
"Just add water, and let me rest!"
While I search for light in darkened spaces,
You sway and smile, with leafy graces!

In your gentle sway, I find my spree,
A dance of laughter, just you and me,
Though life's a jest, and I sometimes cry,
You giggle back, as time slips by!

Oh hint of humor, in your green delight,
You make my troubles feel feather-light,
With petals soft and laughter near,
You're the plant that brings my heart to cheer!

In Praise of Unfurling Grace

Oh dear plant, so green and spry,
You stand so tall, but don't ask why.
With leaves that dance and sway in air,
You're the laziest beauty, yet so rare.

Your blooms unfold with such delight,
Like a surprise party, what a sight!
You sip on water, what a spree,
Where's the punchline? Oh, just let me be!

A guardian of my living space,
In your company, I find my place.
Whenever guests see you at play,
They chuckle, "Look, it's Plant-a-lay!"

So here's to you, my leafy friend,
With you, the laughter never ends.
Your silent jokes and leafy sighs,
Keep me chuckling, oh how time flies!

The Peaceful Bloom's Soft Song

In a pot with a grin so wide,
You chat with dust bunnies at your side.
Your petals whisper secrets fine,
While I just sip my cup of brine.

Your leafy arms, an elegant tease,
Don't mind me, I'm just here to sneeze.
You soak up sun and dodge the heat,
Pretending to be oh-so discreet.

A dance-off with the cat at noon,
You thrive, while I stumble in tune.
But how do you do it, oh so chill?
With each glance, you get the last thrill!

Your soft song fills the cozy room,
A melody that chases gloom.
With laughter, I sing along in jest,
In your presence, I feel truly blessed!

A Lullaby for the Living Room

Close your eyes, the day's at bay,
Here's a plant to make you sway.
With whispers wrapped in leafy cheer,
Who needs a band when you are here?

You sway and sway, but don't you flop,
You take your time, babe, never stop.
Plant songs echo, soft and sweet,
As the couch calls me for a seat.

You giggle with the morning light,
Your giggle makes my worries slight.
As dust bunnies claim their throne,
You nestle in, not alone.

A lullaby that knows no end,
You wear that charm, my leafy friend.
In every room, you're quite the show,
A thriving star, oh don't you know?

Serene Curves of Nature's Art

Look at you, with curves so grand,
Like a supermodel, but you're a plant!
Strutting 'round like you own the floor,
Nature's canvas that I adore.

Your leaves wave "hi" and never pout,
While I juggle snacks and spill 'em out.
Oh peace lily, your soft green grace,
Turns the mess into a lovely place.

You soak in sunlight, ooh what a glow,
While I forget where I placed my toe.
But you don't mind, just sway with me,
A buddy with style, you smile with glee!

So here's my toast, plant dear and wise,
With your green spirit, my heart flies.
In this living room, you reign supreme,
A playful soul, a charming dream!

Blossoms of Serenity

In the corner, green and bright,
Stands a plant that feels just right.
Dust bunnies can't compare,
To this peace with fragrant flair.

Its leaves dance when I walk by,
Makes me feel like I can fly.
Roots in soil, it's got no rush,
Sipping water, in a hush.

With petals white as clouds above,
It makes me skip and sing with love.
I tried to teach it a new trick,
But it just sat there, calm and slick.

Watch it glow in morning light,
Telling worries to take flight.
In my living room it stands,
Always cool; never demands.

Whispered Elegance

This plant's dressed in purest white,
Makes my home feel pure delight.
Winked at me as I walked past,
I swear it's judging me—so fast.

It doesn't pout or scream for sun,
Just sits and laughs, it's having fun.
I think it knows more than I do,
Maybe it thinks I'm a fool too.

Occasionally, it droops a tad,
I rush to give it love—that's rad!
It perks up, giving me a grin,
I'm pretty sure I'm still not winning.

A throne of leaves in every space,
Quietly smiling, full of grace.
Its elegance leaves me in awe,
Still, it won't budge when I saw.

The Calm Within the Bloom

When I'm frazzled, feeling low,
That calm plant puts on a show.
Whispers secrets to the room,
Spreads a vibe that chases gloom.

I water it with all my love,
Oh, peace lily, from above!
It seems to thrive on coffee spills,
Laughing softly through my ills.

I tried to bring it to a party,
But it huffed, "This gets too hearty!"
Now it guards my tranquil space,
Giggling softly, full of grace.

Amidst the hustle, it remains,
A living joke that gently gains.
In its presence, I can't resist,
Feeling peaceful, I persist.

Veiled in Tranquility

A plant so sweet, dressed in white,
Bringing calmness, oh what a sight!
It doesn't complain or need a chat,
Just hangs out, doing this and that.

Veiled in elegance, it's wise,
Knows all my secrets, what a surprise!
Right beside the sunny chair,
It listens close without a care.

Showed up once, all dusty and sad,
Now it's thriving—oh, I'm so glad!
Tells me laughter's a better plan,
Oh peace lily, you really can!

When chaos brews in my abode,
It giggles softly, lightens the load.
With every leaf, it shares its tricks,
Teaching me life's simple picks.

Guardian of Gentle Moments

In the corner, you stand so proud,
With petals like whispers, not too loud.
A guardian for times both goofy and bright,
You dance with the dust in the soft morning light.

Your leaves have a knack for catching my eye,
They somehow agree when I'm feeling shy.
As if to say, 'Hey, no need to fret!'
With you by my side, I'm a fun little pet.

Oh, how you sway when a breeze passes through,
Making silly shapes that remind me of you.
A comedian dressed in botanical grace,
With each little tremor, you bring smiles to face.

So here's to the laughter you freely provide,
A quirky companion, my green-hearted guide.
In moments of stillness, or chaos we seek,
You're the punchline I cherish, with humor unique.

A Reflection in White

In the mirror, a vision of serene delight,
You're an all-white wonder, a beautiful sight.
With petals so glossy, you beam like a star,
A reflection of peace, never too far.

Yet sometimes I think you know more than you show,
As if to whisper secrets, 'Shh, just let it flow.'
Your elegance sways with each quirky breeze,
You giggle at chaos with the greatest of ease.

When friends drop by for a laugh or two,
You seem to smirk, like you know they're a crew.
"Oh look, folks are noisy!" you seem to imply,
While I hide my grin— oh my, oh my!

With you in the room, there's never a need,
For big plans or stunts, just your soft, gentle creed.
You're the quiet punchline of every shared laugh,
A comical moment, a green, leafy half.

The Language of Leaf and Stem

Your leaves tell stories in all kinds of ways,
Like kids on the playground, in bright sunny days.
Twisting and turning, they have tales to share,
Conversations with roots, floating on air.

Sometimes they droop, like they're tired of fun,
Other times they perk up, like, 'I've just begun!'
In your greenness, a message hidden from sight,
"Let's move to the rhythm, keep things light!"

Around you, laughter grows, without any fuss,
Your humor's inclusive, and blended with trust.
"Hey buddy, just breathe!" your foliage might say,
As we chase the mundane, we play and we sway.

So here's to the language you speak every day,
In pranks and in giggles, you warm the highway.
A comedy nestled in each little fold,
In your joyful embrace, life's stories unfold.

Tenderness in Every Fold

Oh, tender friend with your gentle embrace,
You fold like a joke, a soft, funny space.
Each petal a promise of comfort and cheer,
In laughter and whimsy, your essence is clear.

With each little wrinkle, you show us your heart,
Like a mime on a sidewalk, performing a part.
You nod with the rhythm of life as it flows,
Embodied in grace, in your bright, leafy clothes.

A chuckle awaits in the quietest sighs,
You sweet soul of humor, the best of all sighs.
In the late afternoon, with a wink and a swish,
You make the mundane feel like a fun little wish.

So let's raise a glass to your playful finesse,
In the garden of laughter, you're surely the best.
With a nod and a giggle, we'll dance through the day,
For in your tender folds, life's joys find their way.

Resplendence in Simple Elegance

In the corner she stands, all bright and so fair,
A bloom in the shadows, with flair beyond compare.
Her leaves do a dance, like they've drunk a sweet brew,
Whispering secrets that only she knew.

With a wink and a nod, she catches the light,
Making my drab room feel joyous and bright.
Yet when I forget her, she starts to complain,
Drooping her head like a diva in pain.

Each petal a promise, with charm so unique,
In a world full of chaos, she brings out the cheek.
A beauty that giggles, a joke in disguise,
She's the queen of my jungle, with sparkling eyes.

So here's to the green queen, with no need for a crown,
With roots in the soil, she never feels down.
Her elegance simple, her laughter divine,
My sassy companion, forever she'll shine.

The Silent Melody of Green

In the stillness, she hums a soft tune,
Waving her leaves to the light of the moon.
A melody happens in silence so sweet,
With each little sway, she dances on feet.

Her secret life's mission? To thrive and to tease,
With a wink of her leaf, she aims to please.
Sometimes quite sassy, she's not afraid to pout,
When the water is light, she starts to shout out.

Oh, the drama she brings with a simple green hue,
With her blooms looking fine, like a fresh morning dew.
She swirls through the day in a playful embrace,
Turning frowns into laughter, she brightens the place.

So here's to her symphony, loud in its grace,
The peace lily's tune is a marvelous space.
She serenades softly, a silent delight,
In my little green world, she's my star every night.

The Embrace of Nature's Serenity

With her big friendly leaves, she's ready to share,
A cozy warm hug floating here in the air.
She knows all my secrets, they're safe in her fold,
A confidante clad in green, oh so bold!

When life gets too hectic, she whispers, 'Just chill!'
Curl up with a book, let time stand still.
Her laughter erupts as she drinks all my care,
While I sit enchanted in her leafy affair.

She dresses the room in a dress made of grace,
With petals so pure, there's a smile on her face.
Yet distract her too long, and she might just droop,
Turning head down, joining my couch potato troop!

So here's to the peace lady, snazzy and spry,
My partner in calm, as days flutter by.
She's the balm in the chaos, the softest embrace,
In her green, leafy arms, I've found my true space.

Comfort in Every Petal

In a world bustling wild, she stands with a grin,
Each petal a pillow, soft as a din.
She whispers, 'Come close, let's take a break,
Rustle your worries away like a flake.'

With a giggle and rustle in bright morning light,
She shares her soft hints to help everything right.
Her secret ambition? To keep things less tense,
While growing in style, she's got all the sense!

If you want a castle, with comfort galore,
Just bring in the lily, she opens the door.
With petals like pillows, and leaves like a fan,
She's the best therapist, more than any plan.

So grab a warm drink and settle right down,
In her leafy kingdom, shed every frown.
With laughter and love in her leafy abode,
This charming green lady's the best, I've bestowed.

Grace in Each Ruffled Edge

In the corner, she sits all prim,
A plant with a demeanor not so slim.
With leaves like a dance, so finely frayed,
I think she's secretly a diva charade.

Her blooms in white, they wave and tease,
Like fashion models swayed by a breeze.
With every glance, she seems to wink,
"Watch out, room, I'm here! Now link!"

Whenever I water, she gives a sigh,
As if to say, "Oh, do you have to try?"
And when I forget, she droops with flair,
A drama queen without a care.

So here's to the lily, in all her glories,
In the jungle of puns, she's the queen of stories.
With each ruffled edge, she holds a jest,
In the plant world, she surely's the best!

Nature's Poem of Rest

In the sunlight, she sprawls with ease,
Casting shadows that seem to tease.
With stems so straight and leaves that sway,
Who knew plants could have much to say?

She tips and tilts during the day,
Like a lazy cat wanting to play.
"Stop! Right there!" she seems to shout,
"Breath of fresh air, it's what I'm about!"

Her pot is a throne, she rules with grace,
When family visits, she holds her place.
They compliment her, "What a show!"
And I just grin; she steals the show.

So let us laugh at this funny scene,
A plant so sassy, so bright and keen.
In the grand story of nature's best,
She's the punchline and truly blessed!

The Lotus of Inner Peace

In a world of chaos, she stands so still,
Like a wise old sage, oh what a thrill!
With petals that shine, so calm, so bright,
She whispers secrets by day and night.

"Worry not!" she gently coos,
While I stumble in my mismatched shoes.
"Embrace your quirks, just laugh and thrive,"
She's the therapist no one can bribe.

When friends drop by with their ruffled frown,
She greets them kindly, "Let's flip that crown!"
"Life's too short for serious talk,
Join me on this giggle walk!"

So here's to the nectar of joy she brings,
A plant who understands the lighthearted flings.
With each joyful petal that sways in breeze,
I can't help but smile, she makes me feel at ease!

The Soul of the Serene Flora

In the stillness of room, she plays the part,
An actress with a very big heart.
With leaves like fans in her lovely show,
My silent companion, she steals the glow.

She rolls her eyes when I fret and fuss,
"Take it easy, darling, just ride the bus!"
"Let's sip some sunlight, relax for a bit,
Life's too funny; don't throw a fit!"

When friends come over, they joke and cheer,
"Is that a plant or your therapist here?"
With a gentle nod of her leafy crown,
She proves that laughter can wear the frown down.

So here's to the flora that keeps it real,
An evergreen sage with a vibrant zeal.
In her green presence, like a playful breeze,
She sprinkles joy; it's all just a tease!

A Sanctuary's Embrace

In a crowded room, you stand so proud,
A leafy diva, quiet yet loud.
You sip the sunlight, oh what a tease,
With roots that wiggle, and leaves that please.

Dust bunnies tremble beneath your reign,
While you stretch and yawn, cause no one pain.
Tiptoe around as you sip from the air,
You're more of a queen than just a plant in my lair.

With your glossy guard, you make everyone smile,
I swear you could rival the cat with your style.
Strutting your stuff, a pampered delight,
Reducing my worries, making the dark bright.

Keep those blooms coming, oh leafy delight,
With your calm little charm under the moonlight.
You're a weird little wizard, a friend so dear,
Explore the jungle, but let's keep it clear!

In the Presence of Stillness

You sit in the corner, a tranquil sight,
Ignoring the fuss and the noise of the night.
Your silence is louder than any of my chats,
While I'm blabbing away, you're pondering stats.

With a grin on my face, I watch you thrive,
Do you ever trip when you're feeling alive?
With roots in a pot, you've taken a chance,
Always at center stage, ready to dance!

Oh, how you bloom like a proud little star,
Even when my friends insist we drive far.
But you hold the fort, with grace and with style,
Making my life worthwhile, plant-based smile.

In moments of chaos, your calm is so grand,
I raise my glass high for my leafy friend.
Cheers to your leaves, your soft, gentle hue,
In the company of you, I could never feel blue!

The Softest Touch of Green

A gentle giant with leaves so lush,
You keep up with chaos in a silvery hush.
When I trip on the rug, you might just laugh,
You're the snarky sage of my green turf staff.

You hang out in corners, take all my sun,
Hoarding the light, but you're still lots of fun!
With a sprinkle of water, you glisten and glow,
While my cat mopes around, feeling quite low.

My dear leafy friend, you don't take a cue,
From my lute-playing neighbor or misfit crew.
You sway with the music and thrill at the beat,
A peace-loving plant, a botanical feat.

With your elegance flaring and colors so bright,
You're the mightiest muse under soft, twinkling light.
Let's laugh at the sunlight that kisses that skin,
You're the fun and the calm — let the games begin!

Harmony in Petals

In the corner, you'm the study's delight,
Your leaves like applause in an apathy fight.
With each little crease, you present a new game,
A talent for charm, but you never seek fame.

Sipping on moisture, drenching joy,
While my thoughts run wild like a hyper little boy.
You nod at my antics, you spin just a tad,
With a flourish you say, 'I'm not one for sad!'

With blooms that bow like they're taking a bow,
Your style is so classy; you own every vow.
You play peek-a-boo with my quirky bird friends,
Rolling your eyes as the laughter extends.

You're the softest of laughter, the heart in our room,
I raise my glass high, cheering for the bloom.
Cheers to the petals that dance with the breeze,
And the peace that you bring me, oh sweet little tease!

www.ingramcontent.com/pod-product-compliance
Lightning Source LLC
Chambersburg PA
CBHW072132070526
44585CB00016B/1646